$\mathcal{L}$ips are portals,
The eyes tell stories

*L*ips are portals,
The eyes tell stories
*But the eyes are liars

Dondago Bellamy

authorHOUSE®

AuthorHouse™
1663 Liberty Drive
Bloomington, IN 47403
www.authorhouse.com
Phone: 1-800-839-8640

Published by AuthorHouse   03/21/2012

ISBN: 978-1-4685-7192-9 (sc)
ISBN: 978-1-4685-7191-2 (e)

Library of Congress Control Number: 2012905372

Any people depicted in stock imagery provided by Thinkstock are models, and such images are being used for illustrative purposes only.
Certain stock imagery © Thinkstock.

This book is printed on acid-free paper.

Because of the dynamic nature of the Internet, any web addresses or links contained in this book may have changed since publication and may no longer be valid. The views expressed in this work are solely those of the author and do not necessarily reflect the views of the publisher, and the publisher hereby disclaims any responsibility for them.

Contents

Water 1

Footprints 2

Conversing 3

Rivers 4

Shakespeare 5

Heartbreak 6

Stages of our doing 7

The eyes are liars 8

I Cried out for you 9

Experimenting 10

Backwards 11

Delicate 12

A Part of u 13

The After 14

Where do we go from here 15

Cocoons (Being in Love) 17

In a whirl 18

Eyes highs 19

A love poem 21

An interlude 22

Names 23

The Eyes 24

Possibility 25

The Dinner 27

Trap thinking 28

A moment of calm 30

Amongst other things 31

The desired 33

Making a house 34

Images 36

Think about you 37

Math 38

To your memory 41

The Incident 43

Insomniac glory 45

Unborn 46

Roses are Blue 47

He left 48

Tension 49

Lucky ('04) 50

The beach 51

Generation 52

Voiceless 53

Heroes 54

In The beginning 55

About The Author 57

Water

As we grow,

Our bond is tightened

Not by childish desire,

But In a way that has transcended

The previous notion of ourselves

Footprints

Sandwiching impressions under half moons
as the world around us cascades,
Mirroring the sparkles
        in her eyes and mouth,
she says something that can only be timeless;
"I love you too."
Gently, for artichokes like this
        pulling away become tattoos
Along a fresh bed of snowflakes;
Footprints are said to be for the obvious
        Leaving fingers to be walked.
Suggestive hedonism venture
without capital, criticism is of some telling.
doubt the self
doubt the Persevered,
a modification of simple language.
Twinkled flaws well wished

Conversing

[Ringing: phone]
I'll serenade u with spaghetti intentions,
      if you'd be the pages in my manuscript,
  -    making yourself a force
and with the grace of poetry's potential.
I would call u out of place,
if I could imagine being engulfed by the warmth of your smile.
See u r the words without a face,
      the essence of what writing is in mind
& I've been writing u for a while.
Suggestions like make it good but not cliché
R in itself the manifestations.
If you could, picture our eyes
trickle down the intentions of your oh my's
& innocence caressing the Senegal (of your heart)
being the middle.

Rivers

It weighs on me,
      Enforcing travel up and down the deserted.
The grounds respond, winds whistle
Resembling the faint hint of laughter.
I'm transported to another,
      closer to your water.
I drink, bathe, set up shelter within you,
      I call you home.
And As we grow,
      laying may become expected,
So instead of kisses,
I'll write messages in her pillow
(love notes letting her know I'd always be here.)
Syllables each sounding melodic to the sleeping,
words,
I will speak in time.

Shakespeare

I love you in so many ways,
But only those three words catch my imagination.
Is it such a crime,
        for my desires to be worn,
Whether frightful or forward,
        As honest as they are
To confess,
        propose family thru the proper channels.
I love you deeply
That I am shook.
Terrified of rejection,
        the thought alone are ingested with poisoned tips.

I am Romeo,
inspired from a love affair that is all too taboo

Heartbreak

Blacken paths speed senses,

Roses entomb,

enticing the obvious.

Slithering, leaving only gestures like tryst and paramour.

I've only one caught a glimpse

and she was as they described,

Unbearable yet forgivable.

Like a fool, my light only imposed

barely creating, innocence lost,

and it never stopped by my hand.

Stages of our doing

Catching eyes ride up and down our innocence,

We plan to be better.

But like everything else we fall into each other and don't like the company. From mine eyes, it seemed She wanted to be an image and I wanted to be a statement. If you've ever be in love you know exactly what that's like. Most days we wait until the last to say hello. But it doesn't ease a thing. We manage and become ghosts. She says she wants this. I'm not too convinced and find myself in this routine. We fight without words, without fists, I wonder how is it we fight? Maybe we're not in love and we're not compatible. But I've met people who still go beyond coexistence. THERE is something obvious. We've admitted it's broken. The thought of being one instead of two is a serene gesture for me, and for her a thought she regrets. This time she said it would be different, even pleaded she'd be better. *"Give me a chance."* But unto her every day is a chance and she continues to disappoint.

The eyes are liars

No comfort tonight or any other

Maybe if I change

       I'm thinking of all the ways,

to say I'm not thinking of you.

I miss running my fingers through your hair

Or when we kissed

and the little bit of you still lingered.

I let you call me by first name.

Maybe I was too much or not enough.

Either way,

U said you liked me then

I Cried out for you

I cried out for you. I did. Certain your words, presence, would make things right. Your smile is to be what it has always been, inspiring. Our love has fallen, I might be to blame. Sorry I know nothing else. Only how to speak, shout (you call it.) And you always needed it to be about you, yet I lay wounded. But picking up pieces are only useful when there are pieces. There is only me, concrete in being concrete, hard from all this desire. When I look around I only see fragments of promise and not the real thing. I can't be convinced. So when I ask is it all worth it maybe, I expect you tell it different.

Experimenting

I want to feel u read me,

      A grim shot.

Telepathic gestures sent thru text messages, tagged

"Prepare for a second coming."

With no ears words lie silent.,

the walls unstable.

Connections lived and some died.

Like no one else I c u,

Full and satisfied

Backwards

Now writing your name backwards
     You are backwards now.
And your meaning different,
Magnified,
Unlike hardly, the original memory.
For instance,
     You are, who I make you
And nothing else.
So forget
However you pass yourself,
It doesn't count

Delicate

I know you.
We are equals but never told
In the flesh our bodies are complementary
As you sweat I rise
responding as expected
Still, I undress you in parts
Starting with the shoes and ending with the socks,
knowing no limits
How can't I have you
Like so many times before,
In contorted fashion intoxicated glances mimicking the spasm,
Creating splints in our once former selves,
Erasing the known and penciling in new initials.

A Part of u

Strolling in the mist hand in hand,
    We speak gibberish like fools in love,
Simple memorandums built for pausing.
I hear the words slipping off your tongue into open pools,
    I hang there
And picture the moist lips of your indecency,
    As each syllable finds residence,
And we are now again relevant.
Instantly u become clear.
And your shapely inspiration walks next to mine.
I am nothing more than a part of your story.

The After

She is gone. The remaining is the residue.

Sweet cemented lullabies

over a plate of forget me not's.

Rosemary trinkets present a room valiant like

Lady must love perfect.

Where do we go from here

I figured you'd walk away if I let you,

So I held onto what seemed fair.

I smothered you out of desperation

only making it worse

And I'm trying to make sense of the once.

U slept steadily and I toss and turn

Indicating what was to be expected.

I thought for once

Maybe if we'd be a little more giving

Than our differences would make us whole

Whole what,

Whole numbers

looking to be whole, then I must be a half,

Which half?

Half dead,

Half alive,

I feel half a heartbeat;

For a long time it's been this way.

I should've made peace

But I am deserving of something other than death.

Can I be happy I wonder

Does a rainbow intrude and that can be some telling of us

But you never get me

(maybe you don't try)

Or I force it on you.

But I don't know where we go from here.

Cocoons (Being in Love)

Ominous gabbing lay foundations to be written in glory

Siren tickling

She lets herself unfold anyway

Triggering the banshee outpouring

Jazzy gyrations the magnetic Rigorous experimenting,

(A lynching of sorts)

Yanking/twisting/the penetrate

All heard universal

Twitching gestures to endearing bends

mimic the sway, perpetuate the sacred,

And twinkle constellations to name a few

Initially stumbling to overbearing obligations

Glimpses resonate with the empowered

Counting questions between moments but only the inconclusive blurry

Awaiting scars to go hastily

Moving in great flamboyance

In a whirl

She—could—behind
Sand dune vapors blast orchards upright,
Leaving blue and purple motifs.
Gondola dreams
      The parrot(s)—
Soap for the lovers
Requesting flavored aged factions to call.

Craft-less, tonsil, percolate!
& topless follicle peeps the scene.
Hustled face representation
College, and the new now.
Farm unlucky four
The basement self medicates.

Eyes highs

Playing round eyes bout and wildly,

Curvatures of twisting tongue are arranged in order of fancy.

Tangent fools find difficulty in comparison.

An orangutan of adlibs,

     Construct towers

Readers of justice,

I've never heard I love you spoken so black and white.

From birth,

they praise striders of time keeping ability.

Through pens lines and opaque beauty,

we create colors,

that for the most part play a backseat in our imagination.

she . . . loves this

     and he . . . does too.

We look forward and for a moment intertwine,

catching flickers of truth.

Our hearts read easy, listen and play, coming alive and strong

Right now, your name is a whisper in my design

So we indulge in myth and plan for all eternal.

We are obvious like it is wrong and innocent for all that is right.

As we misty eyed massage without intentions

We hope to create perfection,

Knowing oh too well how perfectly

Things are imperfect.

She says:) I'm yours when you're ready.

A love poem

I dream of a seated romp calling,

The broken

Pebble

picture frame

Sort of reminiscent of rich moss

And petunia flavored memento.

U

r my calculus.

An interlude

Melodic tunes gyrate talking jizms for the simple with black on black intentions. She says pull me close, whisper. Thinking of something suave but calculated like

"*u smell like soap*."

Walking is good.

Walking with you is better, walking towards you but never for you is preferred.

It was never about song.

The *Kiss of life* humming in the back, the lump in my throat; "*Can I ask you something?*

Mortals combated and the upper crust set to finesse the shame. I can't sleep. I expect gifts, and I see colors clear as day and I fear it's always been that way. Maybe that's why a bed is always empty.

Names

My name is an alphabet soup of prose and poetry truth telling and secret.

From colored roses our admiration gives us pricks becoming cuts, bruises, baring songs sometimes so haunting, I still c the nightmares. My sensitive eyes distort truth. I hope this is truth telling. I can't fully talk. I want to, I just can't.

I see in the dark well surprisingly, and I finally get it. (English and so necessary) I do wonder who gets to judge whose English is correct since they judge me already. I wish it didn't bother me so much or I could just eat my veggies like a "good boy." I color better. I heart color like nothing else. I feel clone-like, like I've already been something else and can't break from shadow. I blame my distorted color, so I play with words. They don't expect it.

The Eyes

the eyes color worlds of suspicion,
worms lie for historical rhetoric with Greek sometimes too.
Screwballs stick to time shiftless on schedule
Syllable easel and the un-deciphered,
Railways climb for fretful men
As inspiration lays over the encouraged thinker.
Memory is everything to some
They no longer make dinosaurs, their descendent s are lucky.
Twice is light, useless even to good eyes
more reliant than its counterparts.
Hope is the no more telling,
what seems obvious, the beauty is unknown.
Grateful,
for wounded eyes surviving to see the grays.

Possibility

What are the possibilities of being born again Butterflies

To soar about our own criticisms

Placed high on our brows similar to thorn crowns,

To learn more than the fate of a pale faced tombstone.

Written in bold face are children, for once we know we are not sane.

Lost and found are the same.

Keynotes suicide all missed until afterwards

The dance between premonition and kiss.

For the lonely who fights there battle,

Only through analytical gestures commonness is found feeling helpless,

If there was a God?

Serenity granted (for those in real need)

Kids like me whose only desire is for some protection from the lions

Who chase our dreams far away

If there were some real choice

In the romantic sense eunuchs are beautiful

And too less is made of singing.

People jump out of joy whereas men sing out of desperation

The Giving might be a final gasp of human existence

Yet giving up is too easy

The Dinner

A Gallon of hopefuls Gathers
-     a hand selected fork dresses the table and
the portable impressions; they pass. Hand
to hand
the preferable. The vanish,
-     —and the stopwatch continues
non-timing little girls.

Golly lingo
Intoxicates. Walking
thru thresholds
Like a holy
goldfish nestled in a place,
Telling itself to be fatuous.
The passer of an atomic soda. I no longer need
A little harmless pollution

Trap thinking

I think less than I use to

I think more than I want

I think if

Thinking was the thing to do

I'd be good at it

I think how scarred I am to think,

How my thoughts can design something too real for me

I don't think I'm better than anyone

But I think it's not fair either,

The thinking being a prison of mine alone or a gateway of my undoing

I think I like who I am

I think I'm going in some direction

I think I'm still a little afraid of the dark,

I even chose to sleep alone

To think

I choose to not be immortal. Immortality is not a sentence but a thought man chases and nearly hides from

I'm thinking about the significance of a smile

How smiling has once saved me again,

So simple and so casual

The world should smile more, especially on those who need it most

I like to think wherever you are

You are smiling

I can feel you

All of you

smiling

And I'm no longer afraid to be myself

I've gone so far thinking

And my innocence is forward worn in bravery

Thinking has imprisoned

Oh how thinking has planted us

A moment of calm

The tickling cold brushes
Running against warm ample fat
Fragments of the earth are ingested and then released,
The drippings toot and beat to jazzy escaladed skylines
After patted encounters embeds itself within crooked grooves
Flashes of fluorescent pluck at maroon tinted coverings
Initiate reactions and cause the opposite,
a massaging tranquil kiss
The aroma intoxicates from all sides
Man is one again,
Primitive and private, sole and savior
He marvels over his past
Wonders what the future holds
And can't find the strength to be content
He reminds himself of the elements

Amongst other things

How does an angel fall so far from grace
To where no one can spot him?
He to blind
To know what is happening
To proud
To ask for help,
I blame no one
But I do wonder whose fault it is.
He was family
He was lost
Somewhere while we continued to live
And in absence caused chaos
To ask what were we doing.
As his finally breaths poured out from his body
I could feel it under me
Like a sick fulfilling prophecy

The Walls, manila
A cold fish lies & a beep is the indication
so I watch the body stale but not stiffen
& whiskey aromas cloud the once peaceful
     Beep
     Beep

Lending our prayers over the lifeless room
no memories to plaster
nothing to leave of the unknown
but bits and pieces.
His face hard/ marked/ and insignificant
other than the peculiar riding along his forehead
Cold follicles dress him
and it's unclear how old he is.

Frail the night of our first visit till the day he left us;
No more pain

       Beep
       Beep

Plugged in and breathing
hindered by the poisonous organs or the intricacies of heartbreak

so much unknown

The desired

I'll insert images of my lusting, the places, people, women I've been in my nine lives, and my shapely and obvious stretched beyond recognition. The physical can be an indication for only a select few, face telling, the burdens heavy and mine alone. I'm unsure if being unusual is necessary if I already stand out. My actions only can only be small talk to a gibber gabbing fool who really believes "a cup of Joe" is American.

Two come together soak, absorb, and end up with too much as if love were the real enemy. Nothing is more like purgatory then the feeling of the earthly decisions haunting, and taunting, worse, kinda like a tree and not quite holding the same affect. Connections live everywhere. But the eyes are selective. Ideas are created and die and some remain masking. Compassion-less body snatchers kill for optimism and a seat. I say who is ready to be a guide yet so impersonal. Who do we talk about? We talk about you, them, me, and then some. It really seems to be there and not yet all present.

Devil music some say, but only when it blow from the gut and when you can't keep up. I wanted to say it and caught myself. They'll say it for me. They'll say, there he goes, again. Coltrane. On early Sunday passion flaring harmfully, unnaturally, predicting. I worry for the outcome, their outcome, his/her and Why? They do time me. I hope my little can make a difference.

Making a house

Home is not a place

      But a thing

An object for recognition

      The picturesque vision of whimsical wisdom

      The conception of innocence immortalized through golden bonds

where pods learn to become plants.

But home is not easy.

I know uncomfort

I don't know home

I question quite like any other being

And there is no stillness

Only the constant shifting like quite doesn't exist.

If it were raw

      Then walls are cold (& faceless)

      Beds lie hollow

      and sleeping is dying twice.

I think about identity often,

Which arising first body or spirit.

     I am sun

     Warped in decadence

I want to find a sky to rekindle our once affair

And home can be safe

Images

An Adolf gesture across the room buffer to bilingual idiot juice. B Vitamins hints, sometimes whiners but not actors. Catapult service pick up Catholic surface dwellers by day. Dada intentionally spells doom backwards for the erotic. E-coli favors are an easy dialect. Fahrenheit niche formation is interwoven with candlestick opportunities. Gibberish takes time. H.I.V. proposed jihad sparks interest. Picture episodic formations of the Id till death do us part. Joyce bleeds for insomniac glory thru paragraphs. Kabuki jewelry plans a funeral.

A Los Angeles haven is often a day dream. Barefoot mantras obsess over M16 sickness. Noël is nowhere. OCD designs the door. No outlet during Plutonium crisis. Some Q-tips are erasers. Raabee al-thaa-nee, the secular should have company. Saharan mats add decor to the already popular. No more portraits suggesting Tiffany's sentiments. Eunuch doodled blue and white superheroes, do a U-turn. Salute the V-day Memorial OR ELSE. I don't trust and don't see; Wednesday is hiring. X-ray drama, simple fear of a tourist. Destructive Y chromosomes are just reasons. Be a Zebra.

Think about you

Think about you.

Think about yours,

Let them become effusions

Mere guidelines as I write between your lines

Initialing, transcending into what they call open.

I look at you

Become transfixed within your already battered,

Barter my appendages

For a piece of your heart

Surrender and tread in the dangers

Wait, as you delegate

And act on your every instruction.

Quibble a bit. I like that.

You was thirsty

Face fully quenched after.

What were you before

Math

(1)

There are angles for those who can't count

red expectations

My home is a calculator without instructions playing with it.

The obtuse is always watching,

and after all has been added, multiplied and divided,

the remains are train tracks not built for walking.

Instead they practice hate openly

reminding us of selfish pursuits. 1+1

That was yesterday and your habits are now mine. 1 minus 1

I down numbers hoping their whole,

And let the elements operate creating this holy diagram. 4

(2)

If u + me = nothing

Then x is the obvious

How should I make cents,

if subtraction to the def is contact?

People no longer choose to be integers

but they compare themselves.

The enlightened is aligned but math isn't a contest

sometimes operating in tongues like,

Sonia Sanchez calligraphy is ice cream

A dope brother name Leroy smoked on the B-side

I once said June Jordan

But remember, No carrying

(3)

Playing games in base ten maybe 5

What's 30% off authenticity?

I like to think I'm the quite one.

Do a rugby poem for those who can't

Simply braid me 4 this itch

Fractions of a younger woman along radio frequency

And I QUOTE "It's not you, it's me."

The sum of my existence is a tattoo

Maybe a booger, if you ask my sister.

I am supposed to be the solution

To your memory

"he was too young"

& other clichés

Let's call him prodigal

for he was not like himself and more alike then, the others.

I looked

& we never met.

Some call me shorter

but you can chalk it up to her bumble bee humor.

I'd agree to not be a creep

but I fear it's in my nature an accident

or however else you wanna say it.

Be—cool—shawty

For jackets inspire selective infatuation

not like life is crap & other mantras

whichever will fit on any given day.

But I am mischief,

A horned devil in waiting.

I try.

And try not saying I miss you in English

& C where it'll get u

The Incident

AT RISE:
> *A man is at a diner. He is dressed in pink bunny suits.*
> *His prickled face suggests his age. The time of day is*
> *unnecessary, but if you plan to know it is around 1:15*
> *in the morning. In hand is a pen preferably blue ink and*
> *seated in front is a note pad.*

WRITER: Frantic water screaming down a shard of glass esophagus, an Olympian targets a gallop. Sneakers of lavender paste align themselves with reference heroes . . .

> (*Jotting down notes*)

SELF: & . . . a chiseled particle dances on a cloud with the other manila handy ribbon wrapped perfection. A frozen dream or a curtain technique of lies (things people tell themselves in the dark.) Tarnish eyes **A minor** or trampled apologies **B flat**, a room is ridden for dying.

> (*He erases the lines*)

WRITER: staple (Red lipstick cologne) capped with leopard print desire gist to name a few.

SELF: Sonic handshakes reek of black butter.
> (*His eyes fixated over the small handle of a clock*)
Drain handle bard, replacement styles colonoscopy black-bob pointy sockets.
> (*Erasing*)
Sheer retardant narcissist hood rat

WRITER: Digits toxic Irish cream, flowerpot

SELF: checkered nutshell retina tattoo

WRITER: cartoon!

SELF: stubble booger peacock, Subtitle: A bouncing paragraph unhinged and draw string pharmacy.

(*And more scribbling . . .*)

WRITER: Let's play a blue eyed game, no **G's B's N's or MF's** please.

SELF: Pedicure parka shots "*LMAO TTYL*" and other face breakers,

WRITER: a botched silhouette, rubber cold noose crevice.

SELF: "*our bodily good*"

WRITER: news and further gabber, what is honest?

Insomniac glory

On the cusp of your injustice

in

And out,

we meet. Dance. As if it is unnatural.

For once,

wished I wasn't so clumsy

and the intent got it right.

Unborn

Soaking, feeding, drunken personality

edging the addiction in sprints

I WANT TO LIVE

Hormones flood

trapping the sorries.

KIDS

"We're just KIDS"

Roses are Blue

Conjoining the uh's and ah's,

Read me vacant.

Aroused face

Lay between canyon and my nothing.

I hate being called "grippas"

Call me AFRICA

They've already sucked me

He said bleed. And I did.

And watch the coil spring-back

Burning impressions

Flowers ablaze

Singes

Wholes in my innocence

A secrete

Only a few know.

He left

He left, left us

Leaving scratches, teeth marks, lines of telling. Somewhere we fit between semi-colons and paragraphs, yet I understand. I's riding high and reading for a feeling. My sister pretends and my brother just doesn't understand.

He left his prints for us to die. Rusted our dreams with tyrant kisses, loaded compliments, silenced, doing his own thing. More than his impressions are all over, hanging, nestled between our feet, even in the crevices of our identity. We try to outrun him because he left and failed to convey something real. We expect apologies but don't wait on 'em.

He left. Left us.

Tension

A contorted flame first bends around bodies

touching its finishes before triggering the grays you see.

The little bit of our evidence is dulled

And in crossing views, our little bit of *God*

is trampled like something antique.

We shall be graceful, and study hands,

for red is law, torn between promise and bitterness.

Some rain drops further beat the downtrodden

And other cool messages

Become transient in large retrospect.

Lucky ('04)

No rosetta stone for poetry,
Instead you gotta be nimble
Or you're dead.
Some perverted message passed along
And we all ask, are we going to the wake?
"I didn't know'em that well"
If that at all.
We just went to school together,
Graduated the same year
In my only memory
was smug
Head-to-toe,
Even his air was pompous.
None the less
He didn't deserve to be buried by his mom
And his ambitions scattered along the mangled automobile
His friend was driving.
I only mention your name
Cause your grave ain't cold enough
To be forgotten

The beach

Driving.

The horizon stretching,

Feeling the white between my toes,

Beads—crawling—falling

The sun introduces itself,

The first sign of prints

A parade rush to the warm

where fishes seen nibble at ankles

Tall waves cruise thru and over

Baring gifts of the extra burns

Their vicious bites leaves tread marks and tear away tattoos

Open, vastness, smooth with few ripples untamed

A place where man comes to die a little

Be children, invent himself.

These grounds are soft for treading forward

Maybe meeting himself.

Generation

we are the system,

A creative instrument reinforced

lacking.

Children of good or evil

in front of a cake.

thought can be straining

Where time easily teases

as inconvenience

And some.

Voiceless

There aren't enough heroes to keep us afloat

Cold trophies are reminders,

whereas walls hold potential yet remain incomplete

Others look in our reflection. Our eyes are fixed on time

But when time is said and done, look how they paint a man

A monster

Likes it's my fault we are here

Likes it's my fault he left,

Even though he planted himself in wet cement.

I write around him, as if I have the space to carve out my own uniqueness.

A voice sets out to find a home

And does

Heroes

Soft and sullen man

Tall like the moon and ferocious.

You devour earfs

In swift dictation

And demand air of all things!

You've opened rivers of conscious thoughts with simplicity.

You know nothing of my today's,

But enough to know my yesterday needed cleaning.

4 letters and 2 vowels in everyday moving to make names.

Your smile scattered in the minds of the greedy

Sometimes teaching stretched dreams become elastic

And errors can be premonitions of gold.

It is in your shadow

We hope to bare witness to our parallels.

In The beginning

Ideas wrestle young minds

submitting dominoes initiate suicide:

> Somewhere a man becomes a terrorist and a patriot

> A woman a hindrance or explorer

Before finding herself

Making love the very things we hate.

I had a dream too,

And they tried their best to take it

Saying I wasn't good enough,

Mimicking

the others like they were something truly special,

The glorified who holler overlooked

Yet no one believes you.

How are your bars, one of clutter

And mine of possibilities unable to touch the sight of sun.

They make it all. They make no sense and plenty of it

Pennies off these things!

Like everyone else I am expected to make planes

Only a few get to glide thru closed doors.

I wonder why Amiri ain't praised

And Giovanni a suggestion and not a requirement

About The Author

I am the oldest of three born to Carol and Dondago Bellamy Sr. I was born and raised in Jersey City, and at the age of six our parents moved to Maplewood, New Jersey. It was in middle school I began to get involved in sports, running track and playing football. During the time I developed a love for sports. Later I attended Columbia High school and I continued to play football and run track. After graduation I went to Cheney University in Cheney, Pennsylvania before finishing with a BA in Sociology from New Jersey City University. It was there I earned an All-American award for running track.

I've always been a kid with an overly active imagination. I would keep myself entertained for hours coming up with new games and inventing new identities. My eighth grade English teacher introduced me to creative writing and short story writing. As my interests in music grew so did my interest in poetry. I began to write my own mimicking styles of great writers. After writing for a few years and taking some writing courses in college I began to believe writing was something I could make into a career. With the encouragement of family and friends I decided to pursue a dream of writing a book. Lips are portals, eyes tell stories is my first piece and hopefully not my last. Currently I reside in Maplewood, New Jersey.